higher-level thinking Questions

Social Studies

questions by
Miguel Kagan
Christa Chapman
Laurie Kagan

created and designed by
Miguel Kagan

illustrated by
Celso Rodriguez

Kagan

Kagan Publishing
981 Calle Amanecer
San Clemente, CA 92673
(949) 545-6300
Fax: (949) 545-6301
1 (800) 933-2667
www.KaganOnline.com

ISBN: 978-1-879097-50-6

Table of ? Contents

"I had six
honest serving men
They taught me all I knew:
Their names were Where
and What and When
and Why and How and
Who.

— Rudyard Kipling

Higher-Level Thinking Questions for Social Studies
Kagan Publishing • 1 (800) 933-2667 • www.KaganOnline.com

Introduction

In your hands you hold a powerful book. It is a member of a series of transformative blackline activity books. Between the covers, you will find questions, questions, and more questions! But these are no ordinary questions. These are the important kind—higher-level thinking questions—the kind that stretch your students' minds; the kind that release your students' natural curiosity about the world; the kind that rack your students' brains; the kind that instill in your students a sense of wonderment about your curriculum.

But we are getting a bit ahead of ourselves. Let's start from the beginning. Since this is a book of questions, it seems only appropriate for this introduction to pose a few questions—about the book and its underlying educational philosophy. So Mr. Kipling's Six Honest Serving Men, if you will, please lead the way:

What?
What are higher-level thinking questions?

This is a loaded question (as should be all good questions). Using our analytic thinking skills, let's break this question down into two smaller questions: 1) What is higher-level thinking? and 2) What are questions? When we understand the types of thinking skills and the types of questions, we can combine the best of both worlds, crafting beautiful questions to generate the range of higher-level thinking in our students!

Types of Thinking
There are many different types of thinking. Some types of thinking include:

- applying
- associating
- comparing
- contrasting
- defining
- elaborating
- empathizing
- experimenting
- generalizing
- investigating
- making analogies
- planning
- prioritizing
- recalling
- reflecting
- reversing
- sequencing
- summarizing
- synthesizing
- assessing
- augmenting
- connecting
- decision-making
- drawing conclusions
- eliminating
- evaluating
- explaining
- inferring consequences
- inventing
- memorizing
- predicting
- problem-solving
- reducing
- relating
- role-taking
- substituting
- symbolizing
- understanding
- thinking about thinking (metacognition)

This is quite a formidable list. It's nowhere near complete. Thinking is a big, multifaceted phenomenon. Perhaps the most widely recognized system for classifying thinking and classroom questions is Benjamin Bloom's Taxonomy of Thinking Skills. Bloom's Taxonomy classifies thinking skills into six hierarchical levels. It begins with the lower levels of thinking skills and moves up to higher-level thinking skills: 1) Knowledge, 2) Comprehension, 3) Application, 4) Analysis, 5) Synthesis, 6) Evaluation. See Bloom's Taxonomy on the following page.

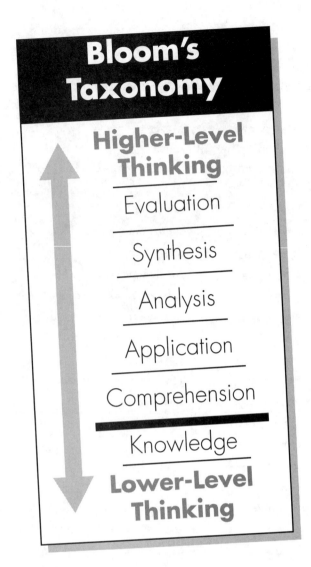

Bloom's Taxonomy

Higher-Level Thinking

Evaluation

Synthesis

Analysis

Application

Comprehension

Knowledge

Lower-Level Thinking

In education, the term "higher-level thinking" often refers to the higher levels of Mr. Bloom's taxonomy. But Bloom's Taxonomy is but one way of organizing and conceptualizing the various types of thinking skills.

There are many ways we can cut the thinking skills pie. We can alternatively view the many different types of thinking skills as, well…many different skills. Some thinking skills may be hierarchical. Some may be interrelated. And some may be relatively independent.

In this book, we take a pragmatic, functional approach. Each type of thinking skill serves a different function. So called "lower-level" thinking skills are very useful for certain purposes. Memorizing and understanding information

are invaluable skills that our students will use throughout their lives. But so too are many of the "higher-level" thinking skills on our list. The more facets of students' thinking skills we develop, the better we prepare them for lifelong success.

Because so much classroom learning heretofore has focused on the "lower rungs" of the thinking skills ladder—knowledge and comprehension, or memorization and understanding—in this series of books we have chosen to focus on questions to generate "higher-level" thinking. This book is an attempt to correct the imbalance in the types of thinking skills developed by classroom questions.

Types of Questions

As we ask questions of our students, we further promote cognitive development when we use Fat questions, Low-Consensus questions, and True questions.

Fat Questions vs. Skinny Questions

Skinny questions are questions that require a skinny answer. For example, after reading a poem, we can ask: "Did you like the poem?" Even though this question could be categorized as an Evaluation question—Bloom's highest level of thinking— it can be answered with one monosyllabic word: "Yes" or "No." How much thinking are we actually generating in our students?

We can reframe this question to make it a fat question: "What things did you like about the poem? What things did you dislike?" Notice no short answer will do. Answering this fattened-up question requires more elaboration. These fat questions presuppose not that there is only one thing but things plural that the student liked and things that she did not like. Making things plural is one way to make skinny questions fat. Students stretch their minds to come up with multiple ideas or solutions. Other easy ways to

Higher-Level Thinking Questions for Social Studies
Kagan Publishing • 1 (800) 933-2667 • www.KaganOnline.com

make questions fat is to add "Why or why not?" or "Explain" or "Describe" or "Defend your position" to the end of a question. These additions promote elaboration beyond a skinny answer. Because language and thought are intimately intertwined, questions that require elaborate responses stretch students' thinking: They grapple to articulate their thoughts.

The type of questions we ask impact not just the type of thinking we develop in our students, but also the depth of thought. Fat questions elicit fat responses. Fat responses develop both depth of thinking and range of thinking skills. The questions in this book are designed to elicit fat responses—deep and varied thinking.

High-Consensus Questions vs. Low-Consensus Questions

A high-consensus question is one to which most people would give the same response, usually a right or wrong answer. After learning about sound, we can ask our students: "What is the name of a room specially designed to improve acoustics for the audience?" This is a high-consensus question. The answer (auditorium) is either correct or incorrect.

Compare the previous question with a low-consensus question: "If you were going to build an auditorium, what special design features would you take into consideration?" Notice, to the low-consensus question there is no right or wrong answer. Each person formulates his or her unique response. To answer, students must apply what they learned, use their ingenuity and creativity.

High-consensus questions promote convergent thinking. With high-consensus questions we strive to direct students **what to think**. Low-consensus questions promote divergent thinking, both critical and creative. With low-consensus

questions we strive to develop students' **ability to think**. The questions in this book are low-consensus questions designed to promote independent, critical and creative thought.

True Questions vs. Review Questions

We all know what review questions are. They're the ones in the back of every chapter and unit. Review questions ask students to regurgitate previously stated or learned information. For example, after learning about the rain forest we may ask: "What percent of the world's oxygen does the rain forest produce?" Students can go back a few pages in their books or into their memory banks and pull out the answer. This is great if we are working on memorization skills, but does little to develop "higher-order" thinking skills.

True questions, on the other hand, are meaningful questions—questions to which we do not know the answer. For example: "What might happen if all the world's rain forests were cut down?" This is a hypothetical; we don't know the answer but considering the question forces us to think. We infer some logical consequences based on what we know. The goal of true questions is not a correct answer, but the thinking journey students take to create a meaningful response. True questions are more representative of real life. Seldom is there a black and white answer. In life, we struggle with ambiguity, confounding variables, and uncertain outcomes. There are millions of shades of gray. True questions prepare students to deal with life's uncertainties.

When we ask a review question, we know the answer and are checking to see if the student does also. When we ask a true question, it is truly a question. We don't necessarily know the answer and neither does the student. True questions are

> **Education is not the filling of a pail, but the lighting of a fire.**
>
> — William Butler Yeats

Types of Questions

Skinny ⟶ **Fat**
- Short Answer
- Shallow Thinking

- Elaborated Answer
- Deep Thinking

High-Consensus ⟶ **Low-Consensus**
- Right or Wrong Answer
- Develops Convergent Thinking
- "What" to Think

- No Single Correct Answer
- Develops Divergent Thinking
- "How" to Think

Review ⟶ **True**
- Asker Knows Answer
- Checking for Correctness

- Asker Doesn't Know Answer
- Invitation to Think

often an invitation to think, ponder, speculate, and engage in a questioning process.

We can use true questions in the classroom to make our curriculum more personally meaningful, to promote investigation, and awaken students' sense of awe and wonderment in what we teach. Many questions you will find in this book are true questions designed to make the content provocative, intriguing, and personally relevant.

The box above summarizes the different types of questions. The questions you will find in this book are a move away from skinny, high-consensus, review questions toward fat, low-consensus true questions. As we ask these types of questions in our class, we transform even mundane content into a springboard for higher-level thinking. As we integrate these question gems into our daily lessons, we create powerful learning experiences. ***We do not fill our students' pails with knowledge; we kindle their fires to become lifetime thinkers.***

 **Why?** Why should I use higher-level thinking questions in my classroom?

As we enter the new millennium, major shifts in our economic structure are changing the ways we work and live. The direction is increasingly toward an information-based, high-tech economy. The sum of our technological information is exploding. We could give you a figure how rapidly information is doubling, but by the time you read this, the number would be outdated! No kidding.

But this is no surprise. This is our daily reality. We see it around us everyday and on the news: cloning, gene manipulation, e-mail, the Internet, Mars rovers, electric cars, hybrids, laser surgery, CD-ROMs, DVDs. All around us we see the wheels of progress turning: New discoveries, new technologies, a new societal knowledge and information base. New jobs are being created

6

today in fields that simply didn't exist yesterday.

How do we best prepare our students for this uncertain future—a future in which the only constant will be change? As we are propelled into a world of ever-increasing change, what is the relative value of teaching students facts versus thinking skills? This point becomes even more salient when we realize that students cannot master everything, and many facts will soon become obsolete. Facts become outdated or irrelevant. Thinking skills are for a lifetime. Increasingly, how we define educational success will be away from the quantity of information mastered. Instead, we will define success as our students' ability to generate questions, apply, synthesize, predict, evaluate, compare, categorize.

If we as a professionals are to proactively respond to these societal shifts, thinking skills will become central to our curriculum. Whether we teach thinking skills directly, or we integrate them into our curriculum, the power to think is the greatest gift we can give our students!

We believe the questions you will find in this book are a step in the direction of preparing students for lifelong success. The goal is to develop independent thinkers who are critical and creative, regardless of the content. We hope the books in this series are more than sets of questions. We provide them as a model approach to questioning in the classroom.

On pages 8 and 9, you will find Questions to Engage Students' Thinking Skills. These pages contain numerous types of thinking and questions designed to engage each thinking skill. As you make your own questions for your students with your own content, use these question starters to help you frame

> **Virtually the only predictable trend is continuing change.**
> — Dr. Linda Tsantis, Creating the Future

your questions to stimulate various facets of your students' thinking skills. Also let your students use these question starters to generate their own higher-level thinking questions about the curriculum.

Who?
Who is this book for?

This book is for you and your students, but mostly for your students. It is designed to help make your job easier. Inside you will find hundreds of ready-to-use reproducible questions. Sometimes in the press for time we opt for what is easy over what is best. These books attempt to make easy what is best. In this treasure chest, you will find hours and hours of timesaving ready-made questions and activities.

Place Higher-Level Thinking In Your Students' Hands

As previously mentioned, this book is even more for your students than for you. As teachers, we ask a tremendous number of questions. Primary teachers ask 3.5 to 6.5 questions per minute! Elementary teachers average 348 questions a day. How many questions would you predict our students ask? Researchers asked this question. What they found was shocking: Typical students ask approximately one question per month.* One question per month!

Although this study may not be representative of your classroom, it does suggest that in general, as teachers we are missing out on a very powerful force—student-generated questions. The capacity to answer higher-level thinking questions is

* Myra & David Sadker, "Questioning Skills" in *Classroom Teaching Skills*, 2nd ed. Lexington, MA: D.C. Heath & Co., 1982.

Questions to Engage Students' Thinking Skills

Analyzing
- How could you break down…?
- What components…?
- What qualities/characteristics…?

Applying
- How is ____ an example of…?
- What practical applications…?
- What examples…?
- How could you use…?
- How does this apply to…?
- In your life, how would you apply…?

Assessing
- By what criteria would you assess…?
- What grade would you give…?
- How could you improve…?

Augmenting/Elaborating
- What ideas might you add to…?
- What more can you say about…?

Categorizing/Classifying/Organizing
- How might you classify…?
- If you were going to categorize…?

Comparing/Contrasting
- How would you compare…?
- What similarities…?
- What are the differences between…?
- How is ____ different…?

Connecting/Associating
- What do you already know about…?
- What connections can you make between…?
- What things do you think of when you think of…?

Decision-Making
- How would you decide…?
- If you had to choose between…?

Defining
- How would you define…?
- In your own words, what is…?

Describing/Summarizing
- How could you describe/summarize…?
- If you were a reporter, how would you describe…?

Determining Cause/Effect
- What is the cause of…?
- How does ____ effect ____?
- What impact might…?

Drawing Conclusions/ Inferring Consequences
- What conclusions can you draw from…?
- What would happen if…?
- What would have happened if…?
- If you changed ____, what might happen?

Eliminating
- What part of ____ might you eliminate?
- How could you get rid of…?

Evaluating
- What is your opinion about…?
- Do you prefer…?
- Would you rather…?
- What is your favorite…?
- Do you agree or disagree…?
- What are the positive and negative aspects of…?
- What are the advantages and disadvantages…?
- If you were a judge…?
- On a scale of 1 to 10, how would you rate…?
- What is the most important…?
- Is it better or worse…?

Explaining
- How can you explain…?
- What factors might explain…?

Higher-Level Thinking Questions for Social Studies
Kagan Publishing • 1 (800) 933-2667 • www.KaganOnline.com

Experimenting
- How could you test…?
- What experiment could you do to…?

Generalizing
- What general rule can…?
- What principle could you apply…?
- What can you say about all…?

Interpreting
- Why is _____ important?
- What is the significance of…?
- What role…?
- What is the moral of…?

Inventing
- What could you invent to…?
- What machine could…?

Investigating
- How could you find out more about…?
- If you wanted to know about…?

Making Analogies
- How is _____ like _____?
- What analogy can you invent for…?

Observing
- What observations did you make about…?
- What changes…?

Patterning
- What patterns can you find…?
- How would you describe the organization of…?

Planning
- What preparations would you…?

Predicting/Hypothesizing
- What would you predict…?
- What is your theory about…?
- If you were going to guess…?

Prioritizing
- What is more important…?
- How might you prioritize…?

Problem-Solving
- How would you approach the problem?
- What are some possible solutions to…?

Reducing/Simplifying
- In a word, how would you describe…?
- How can you simplify…?

Reflecting/Metacognition
- What would you think if…?
- How can you describe what you were thinking when…?

Relating
- How is _____ related to _____?
- What is the relationship between…?
- How does _____ depend on _____?

Reversing/Inversing
- What is the opposite of…?

Role-Taking/Empathizing
- If you were (someone/something else)…?
- How would you feel if…?

Sequencing
- How could you sequence…?
- What steps are involved in…?

Substituting
- What could have been used instead of…?
- What else could you use for…?
- What might you substitute for…?
- What is another way…?

Symbolizing
- How could you draw…?
- What symbol best represents…?

Synthesizing
- How could you combine…?
- What could you put together…?

a wonderful skill we can give our students, as is the skill to solve problems. Arguably more important skills are the ability to find problems to solve and formulate questions to answer. If we look at the great thinkers of the world—the Einsteins, the Edisons, the Freuds—their thinking is marked by a yearning to solve tremendous questions and problems. It is this questioning process that distinguishes those who illuminate and create our world from those who merely accept it.

Make Learning an Interactive Process

Higher-level thinking is not just something that occurs between students' ears! Students benefit from an interactive process. This basic premise underlies the majority of activities you will find in this book.

As students discuss questions and listen to others, they are confronted with differing perspectives and are pushed to articulate their own thinking well beyond the level they could attain on their own. Students too have an enormous capacity to mediate each other's learning. When we heterogeneously group students to work together, we create an environment to move students through their zone of proximal development. We also provide opportunities for tutoring and leadership. Verbal interaction with peers in cooperative groups adds a dimension to questions not available with whole-class questions and answers.

> **Asking a good question requires students to think harder than giving a good answer.**
>
> — Robert Fisher,
> Teaching Children
> to Learn

Reflect on this analogy: If we wanted to teach our students to catch and throw, we could bring in one tennis ball and take turns throwing it to each student and having them throw it back to us. Alternatively, we could bring in twenty balls and have our students form small groups and have them toss the ball back and forth to each other. Picture the two classrooms: One with twenty balls being caught at any one moment, and the other with just one. In which class would students better and more quickly learn to catch and throw?

The same is true with thinking skills. When we make our students more active participants in the learning process, they are given dramatically more opportunities to produce their own thought and to strengthen their own thinking skills. Would you rather have one question being asked and answered at any one moment in your class, or twenty? Small groups mean more questioning and more thinking. Instead of rarely answering a teacher question or rarely generating their own question, asking and answering questions becomes a regular part of your students' day. It is through cooperative interaction that we truly turn our classroom into a higher-level think tank. The associated personal and social benefits are invaluable.

When?
When do I use higher-level thinking questions?

Do I use these questions at the beginning of the lesson, during the lesson, or after? The answer, of course, is all of the above.

Use these questions or your own thinking questions at the beginning of the lesson to provide a motivational set for the lesson. Pique students' interest about the content with some provocative questions: "What would happen if we didn't have gravity?" "Why did Pilgrims get along with some Native Americans, but not others?" "What do you think this book will be about?" Make the content personally relevant by bringing in students' own knowledge, experiences, and feelings about the content: "What do you know about spiders?" "What things do you like about mystery stories?" "How would you feel if explorers invaded your land and killed your family?" "What do you wonder about electricity?"

Use the higher-level thinking questions throughout your lessons. Use the many questions and activities in this book not as a replacement of your curriculum, but as an additional avenue to explore the content and stretch students' thinking skills.

Use the questions after your lesson. Use the higher-level thinking questions, a journal writing activity, or the question starters as an extension activity to your lesson or unit.

Or just use the questions as stand-alone sponge activities for students or teams who have finished their work and need a challenging project to work on.

It doesn't matter when you use them, just use them frequently. As questioning becomes a habitual part of the classroom day, students' fear of asking silly questions is diminished. As the ancient Chinese proverb states, "Those who ask a silly question may seem a fool for five minutes, but those who do not ask remain a fool for life."

> ## The important thing is to never stop questioning.
> — Albert Einstein

As teachers, we should make a conscious effort to ensure that a portion of the many questions we ask on a daily basis are those that move our students beyond rote memorization. When we integrate higher-level thinking questions into our daily lessons, we transform our role from transmitters of knowledge to engineers of learning.

Where?
Where should I keep this book?

Keep it close by. Inside there are 16 sets of questions. Pull it out any time you teach these topics or need a quick, easy, fun activity or journal writing topic.

How?
How do I get the most out of this book?

In this book you will find 16 topics arranged alphabetically. For each topic there are reproducible pages for: 1) 16 Question Cards, 2) a Journal Writing activity page, 3) and a Question Starters activity page.

1. Question Cards

The Question Cards are truly the heart of this book. There are numerous ways the Question Cards can be used. After the other activity pages are introduced, you will find a description of a variety of engaging formats to use the Question Cards.

Specific and General Questions

Some of the questions provided in this book series are content-specific and others are content-free. For example, the literature questions in the Literature books are content-specific. Questions for the Great Kapok Tree deal specifically with that literature selection. Some language arts questions in the Language Arts book, on the other hand, are content-free. They are general questions that can be used over and over again with new content. For example, the Book Review questions can be used after reading any book. The Story Structure questions can be used after reading any story. You can tell by glancing at the title of the set and some of the questions whether the set is content-specific or content-free.

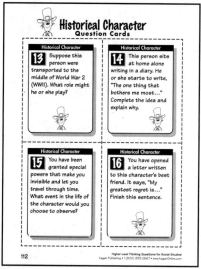

A Little Disclaimer

Not all of the "questions" on the Question Cards are actually questions. Some instruct students to do something. For example, "Compare and contrast…" We can also use these directives to develop the various facets of students' thinking skills.

The Power of Think Time

As you and your students use these questions, don't forget about the power of Think Time! There are two different think times. The first is the time between the question and the response. The second is the time between the response and feedback on the response. Think time has been shown to greatly enhance the quality of student thinking. If students are not pausing for either think time, or doing it too briefly, emphasize its importance. Five little seconds of silent think time after the question and five more seconds before feedback are proven, powerful ways to promote higher-level thinking in your class.

Use Your Question Cards for Years

For attractive Question Cards that will last for years, photocopy them on color card-stock paper and laminate them. To save time, have the Materials Monitor from each team pick up one card set, a pair of scissors for the team, and an envelope or rubber band. Each team cuts out their own set of Question Cards. When they are done with the activity, students can place the Question Cards in the envelope and write the name of the set on the envelope or wrap the cards with a rubber band for storage.

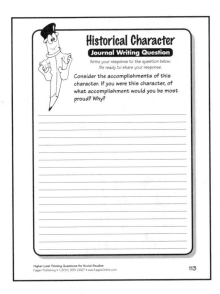

2. Journal Question

The Journal Writing page contains one of the 16 questions as a journal writing prompt. You can substitute any question, or use one of your own. The power of journal writing cannot be overstated. The act of writing takes longer than speaking and thinking. It allows the brain time to make deep connections to the content. Writing requires the writer to present his or her response in a clear, concise language. Writing develops both strong thinking and communication skills.

A helpful activity before journal writing is to have students discuss the question in pairs or in small teams. Students discuss their ideas and what they plan to write. This little prewriting activity ignites ideas for those students who stare blankly at their Journal Writing page. The interpersonal interaction further helps students articulate what they are thinking about the topic and invites students to delve deeper into the topic.

Tell students before they write that they will share their journal entries with a partner or with their team. This motivates many students to improve their entry. Sharing written responses also promotes flexible thinking with open-ended questions, and allows students to hear their peers' responses, ideas and writing styles.

Have students keep a collection of their journal entries in a three-ring binder. This way you can collect them if you wish for assessment or have students go back to reflect on their own learning. If you are using questions across the curriculum, each subject can have its own journal or own section within the binder. Use the provided blackline on the following page for a cover for students' journals or have students design their own.

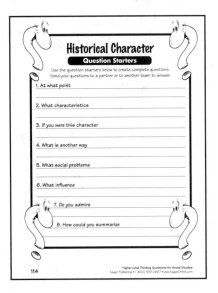

3. Question Starters

The Question Starters activity page is designed to put the questions in the hands of your students. Use these question starters to scaffold your students' ability to write their own thinking questions. This page includes eight question starters to direct students to generate questions across the levels and types of thinking. This Question Starters activity page can be used in a few different ways:

Individual Questions

Have students independently come up with their own questions. When done, they can trade their questions with a partner. On a separate sheet of paper students answer their partners' questions. After answering, partners can share how they answered each other's questions.

JOURNAL

My Best Thinking

This Journal Belongs to

Higher-Level Thinking Questions for Social Studies
Kagan Publishing • 1 (800) 933-2667 • www.KaganOnline.com

Pair Questions

Students work in pairs to generate questions to send to another pair. Partners take turns writing each question and also take turns recording each answer. After answering, pairs pair up to share how they answered each other's questions.

Team Questions

Students work in teams to generate questions to send to another team. Teammates take turns writing each question and recording each answer. After answering, teams pair up to share how they answered each other's questions.

Teacher-Led Questions

For young students, lead the whole class in coming up with good higher-level thinking questions.

Teach Your Students About Thinking and Questions

An effective tool to improve students' thinking skills is to teach students about the types of thinking skills and types of questions. Teaching students about the types of thinking skills improves their metacognitive abilities. When students are aware of the types of thinking, they may more effectively plan, monitor, and evaluate their own thinking. When students understand the types of questions and the basics of question construction, they are more likely to create effective higher-level thinking questions. In doing so they develop their own thinking skills and the thinking of classmates as they work to answer each other's questions.

Table of Activities

The Question Cards can be used in a variety of game-like formats to forge students' thinking skills. They can be used for cooperative team and pair work, for whole-class questioning, for independent activities, or at learning centers. On the following pages you will find numerous excellent options to use your Question Cards. As you use the Question Cards in this book, try the different activities listed below to add novelty and variety to the higher-level thinking process.

Activities

team activity #1

Question Commander

Preferably in teams of four, students shuffle their Question Cards and place them in a stack, questions facing down, so that all teammates can easily reach the Question Cards. Give each team a Question Commander set of instructions (blackline provided on following page) to lead them through each question.

Student One becomes the Question Commander for the first question. The Question Commander reads the question aloud to the team, then asks the teammates to think about the question and how they would answer it. After the think time, the Question Commander selects a teammate to answer the question. The Question Commander can spin a spinner or roll a die to select who will answer. After the teammate gives the answer, Question Commander again calls for think time, this time asking the team to think about the answer. After the think time, the Question Commander leads a team

discussion in which any teammember can contribute his or her thoughts or ideas to the question, or give praise or reactions to the answer.

When the discussion is over, Student Two becomes the Question Commander for the next question.

Question Commander
Instruction Cards

Question Commander

1. Ask the Question:
Question Commander reads the question to the team.
2. Think Time: "Think of your best answer."
3. Answer the Question: The Question Commander selects a teammate to answer the question.
4. Think Time: "Think about how you would answer differently or add to the answer."
5. Team Discussion: As a team, discuss other possible answers or reactions to the answer given.

Question Commander

1. Ask the Question:
Question Commander reads the question to the team.
2. Think Time: "Think of your best answer."
3. Answer the Question: The Question Commander selects a teammate to answer the question.
4. Think Time: "Think about how you would answer differently or add to the answer."
5. Team Discussion: As a team, discuss other possible answers or reactions to the answer given.

Question Commander

1. Ask the Question:
Question Commander reads the question to the team.
2. Think Time: "Think of your best answer."
3. Answer the Question: The Question Commander selects a teammate to answer the question.
4. Think Time: "Think about how you would answer differently or add to the answer."
5. Team Discussion: As a team, discuss other possible answers or reactions to the answer given.

Question Commander

1. Ask the Question:
Question Commander reads the question to the team.
2. Think Time: "Think of your best answer."
3. Answer the Question: The Question Commander selects a teammate to answer the question.
4. Think Time: "Think about how you would answer differently or add to the answer."
5. Team Discussion: As a team, discuss other possible answers or reactions to the answer given.

Fan-N-Pick

In a team of four, Student One fans out the question cards, and says, "Pick a card, any card!" Student Two picks a card and reads the question out loud to teammates. After five seconds of think time, Student Three gives his or her answer. After another five seconds of think time, Student Four paraphrases, praises, or adds to the answer given. Students rotate roles for each new round.

Spin-N-Think™

Spin-N-Think spinners are available from Kagan to lead teams through the steps of higher-level thinking. Students spin the Spin-N-Think™ spinner to select a student at each stage of the questioning to: 1) ask the question, 2) answer the question, 3) paraphrase and praise the answer, 4) augment the answer, and 5) discuss the question or answer. The Spin-N-Think™ game makes higher-level thinking more fun, and holds students accountable because they are often called upon, but never know when their number will come up.

Three-Step Interview

After the question is read to the team, students pair up. The first step is an interview in which one student interviews the other about the question. In the second step, students remain with their partner but switch roles: The interviewer becomes the interviewee. In the third step, the pairs come back together and each student in turn presents to the team what their partner shared. Three-Step Interview is strong for individual accountability, active listening, and paraphrasing skills.

Team Discussion

Team Discussion is an easy and informal way of processing the questions: Students read a question and then throw it open for discussion. Team Discussion, however, does not ensure that there is individual accountability or equal participation.

Think-Pair-Square

One student reads a question out loud to teammates. Partners on the same side of the table then pair up to discuss the question and their answers. Then, all four students come together for an open discussion about the question.

Question-Write-RoundRobin

Students take turns asking the team the question. After each question is asked, each student writes his or her ideas on a piece of paper. After students have finished writing, in turn they share their ideas. This format creates strong individual accountability because each student is expected to develop and share an answer for every question.

Mix-Pair-Discuss

Each student gets a different Question Card. For 16 to 32 students, use two sets of questions. In this case, some students may have the same question which is OK. Students get out of their seats and mix around the classroom. They pair up with a partner. One partner reads his or her Question Card and the other answers. Then they switch roles. When done they trade cards and find a new partner. The process is repeated for a predetermined amount of time. The rule is students cannot pair up with the same partner twice. Students may get the same questions twice or more, but each time it is with a new partner. This strategy is a fun, energizing way to ask and answer questions.

Think-Pair-Share

Think-Pair-Share is teacher-directed. The teacher asks the question, then gives students think time. Students then pair up to share their thoughts about the question. After the pair discussion, one student is called on to share with the class what was shared in his or her pair. Think-Pair-Share does not provide as much active participation for students as Think-Pair-Square because only one student is called upon at a time, but is a nice way to do whole-class sharing.

Inside-Outside Circle

Each student gets a Question Card. Half of the students form a circle facing out. The other half forms a circle around the inside circle; each student in the outside circle faces one student in the inside circle. Students in the outside circle ask inside circle students a question. After the inside circle students answer the question, students switch roles questioning and answering. After both have asked and answered a question, they each praise the other's answers and then hold up a hand indicating they are finished. When most students have a hand up, have students trade cards with their partner and rotate to a new partner. To rotate, tell the outside circle to move to the left. This format is a lively and enjoyable way to ask questions and have students listen to the thinking of many classmates.

Question & Answer

This might sound familiar: Instead of giving students the Question Cards, the teacher asks the questions and calls on one student at a time to answer. This traditional format eliminates simultaneous, cooperative interaction, but may be good for introducing younger students to higher-level questions.

Numbered Heads Together

Students number off in their teams so that every student has a number. The teacher asks a question. Students put their "heads together" to discuss the question. The teacher then calls on a number and selects a student with that number to share what his or her team discussed.

pair activity #1

RallyRobin

Each pair gets a set of Question Cards. Student A in the pair reads the question out loud to his or her partner. Student B answers. Partners take turns asking and answering each question.

Pair Discussion

Partners take turns asking the question. The pair then discusses the answer together. Unlike RallyRobin, students discuss the answer. Both students contribute to answering and to discussing each other's ideas.

Question-Write-Share-Discuss

One partner reads the Question Card out loud to his or her teammate. Both students write down their ideas. Partners take turns sharing what they wrote. Partners discuss how their ideas are similar and different.

Journal Writing

Students pick one Question Card and make a journal entry or use the question as the prompt for an essay or creative writing. Have students share their writing with a partner or in turn with teammates.

Independent Answers

Students each get their own set of Questions Cards. Pairs or teams can share a set of questions, or the questions can be written on the board or put on the overhead projector. Students work by themselves to answer the questions on a separate sheet of paper. When done, students can compare their answers with a partner, teammates, or the whole class.

Center Ideas

1. Question Card Center

At one center, have the Question Cards and a Spin-N-Think™ spinner, Question Commander instruction card, or Fan-N-Pick instructions. Students lead themselves through the thinking questions. For individual accountability, have each student record their own answer for each question.

2. Journal Writing Center

At a second center, have a Journal Writing activity page for each student. Students can discuss the question with others at their center, then write their own journal entry. After everyone is done writing, students share what they wrote with other students at their center.

3. Question Starters Center

At a third center, have a Question Starters page. Split the students at the center into two groups. Have both groups create thinking questions using the Question Starters activity page. When the groups are done writing their questions, they trade questions with the other group at their center. When done answering each other's questions, two groups pair up to compare their answers.

Higher-Level Thinking Questions for Social Studies
Kagan Publishing • 1 (800) 933-2667 • www.KaganOnline.com

Bill of Rights

higher-level thinking questions

Congress shall make no law respecting an establishment of religion, or prohibiting the free exercise thereof; or abridging the freedom of speech, or of the press; or the right of the people peaceably to assemble, and to petition the government for a redress of grievances.

— Amendment 1, 1791

Higher-Level Thinking Questions for Social Studies
Kagan Publishing • 1 (800) 933-2667 • www.KaganOnline.com

Bill of Rights
Question Cards

Bill of Rights

1 Why do you think the first 10 amendments to the constitution are called the "Bill of Rights?" What might be another good name?

Bill of Rights

2 The second amendment guarantees people the right to bear arms. Congress has since outlawed machine guns, sawed-off shotguns, and assault rifles. Is this fair? Why or why not?

Bill of Rights

3 Why is it important that Congress cannot keep people from speaking or writing what they think?

Bill of Rights

4 If there is freedom of speech, why are movies often edited for television and swearing and obscene content not allowed on the radio?

Bill of Rights
Question Cards

5 What do you think would happen if Congress tried to establish an official religion?

6 The fourth amendment states that people cannot be arrested or searched without "probable cause." If you were a judge who issued search warrants, how would you interpret probable cause?

7 If a person is found not guilty, but evidence against him or her is found at a later date, should he or she be tried again? Why or why not?

8 Why is it important that people who are accused have the right to be represented by a lawyer?

30

Bill of Rights
Question Cards

Bill of Rights

9 The eighth amendment says people should not have to suffer cruel or unusual punishment. What would you consider "cruel or unusual punishment?"

Bill of Rights

10 The seventh amendment guarantees people in federal courts the right to a jury trial. If a judge disagrees with the jury, should he or she be allowed to overturn the verdict?

Bill of Rights

11 If you were going to add an eleventh amendment to the Bill of Rights, what would it say?

Bill of Rights

12 If we had no Bill of Rights, how would the United States be different?

Bill of Rights

13 If someone is in a criminal case, why shouldn't he or she be forced to say anything that could convict him or her?

Bill of Rights

14 If the government wanted to build a freeway where your house is, should they be allowed to take your house? Why or why not?

Bill of Rights

15 Why is it important to have speedy and public trials with a local jury?

Bill of Rights

16 The third amendment says that in time of peace, citizens cannot be forced to provide a place in their house for a soldier. Even in wartime, this can only be done if it is accordance with the law. How applicable is this amendment to us today? Should it be removed?

Bill of Rights

Journal Writing Question

Write your response to the question below.
Be ready to share your response.

If you were going to add an eleventh amendment to the Bill of Rights, what would it say?

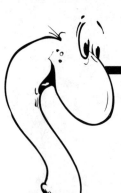

Bill of Rights

Use the question starters below to create complete questions.
Send your questions to a partner or to another team to answer.

1. What is the importance

2. What commonalities

3. How successful

4. Is the first amendment

5. How could you improve

6. Why did the writers

7. How would you describe

8. If you could eliminate

Higher-Level Thinking Questions for Social Studies
Kagan Publishing • 1 (800) 933-2667 • www.KaganOnline.com

Careers and Work

higher-level thinking questions

"Every thought we think is creating our future.

— Louise L. Hay

Careers and Work
Question Cards

Careers and Work

1 What do you want to be when you grow up? Why?

Careers and Work

2 Name the three worst jobs you can imagine. What makes them so bad?

Careers and Work

3 Is it more important to love what you do or to make a lot of money? Explain.

Careers and Work

4 Do you think it's fair that athletes and actors often make much more money than the President? Why or why not?

Careers and Work

5 Name one job that requires a lot of education. Why do you think it takes so much schooling?

Careers and Work

6 In your opinion, what is the most important job in your community?

Careers and Work

7 What do your mom and/or dad do for work? Would you like to have one of their jobs? Why or why not?

Careers and Work

8 Should illegal aliens be allowed to work? Why or why not?

Careers and Work
Question Cards

Careers and Work

9 Should there be a minimum age for working? If so, what should the minimum age be? Should that age apply to all types of work? What should the retirement age be?

Careers and Work

10 Should there be a minimum wage or should the boss and the worker be allowed to agree on whatever they think is fair?

Careers and Work

11 Should small businesses get special treatment from the government or should all businesses get treated equally?

Careers and Work

12 What would you do if there were no jobs left when you finished with your education?

Careers and Work
Question Cards

Careers and Work

13 Should sex, age, or ethnicity ever be taken into account when determining pay? Explain your position.

Careers and Work

14 Would you rather work all day and have your nights free or work all night and have your days free? Explain.

Careers and Work

15 Should people get more benefits the longer they have a job, or should everyone be treated equally? Why?

Careers and Work

16 Today, it is much more common that both the husband and the wife work than in the past. What are the advantages and disadvantages of both working?

Higher-Level Thinking Questions for Social Studies
Kagan Publishing • 1 (800) 933-2667 • www.KaganOnline.com

Careers and Work

Journal Writing Question

Write your response to the question below.
Be ready to share your response.

**What do you want to be when you grow up?
Why?**

_____

_____
_____

_____
_____
_____
_____
_____
_____
_____
_____
_____
_____
_____
_____
_____
_____
_____
_____
_____
_____

Careers and Work

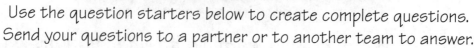
Question Starters

Use the question starters below to create complete questions.
Send your questions to a partner or to another team to answer.

1. If you owned a company _____

_____

2. If people didn't work _____

_____

3. What role _____

_____

4. What kind of job _____

_____

5. What preparations _____

_____

6. Should the boss _____

_____

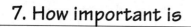   7. How important is _____

_____

8. How would you feel if _____

_____

Higher-Level Thinking Questions for Social Studies
Kagan Publishing • 1 (800) 933-2667 • www.KaganOnline.com

Community

higher-level thinking questions

"Those having torches will pass them on to others.

— Plato

Community
Question Cards

Community

1 Complete the following sentence. "Our community is…"

Community

2 You are nominated as the new chairperson for your community's Improvement Committee. What one thing would you change about your community? Why?

Community

3 If you had a friend or relative come to visit from out of town and wanted a tour, where would you take him or her?

Community

4 How would you describe the people in your community? Are the members of your community more similar or more different? Explain.

Community
Question Cards

5 What is something special your community is known for or what would you like your community to be known for?

6 What is one thing you love about your community? Describe it.

7 Would you rather live somewhere else or stay in your community? Explain.

8 What general statements can you make about your community based on your experience?

Community
Question Cards

Community

9 Do you live in a big or small community? What are three advantages and three disadvantages of living in a community your size?

Community

10 Would you rather live in a more urban (more city) or a more rural (more country) community? Why?

Community

11 How has your community changed over time? What do you think it might have been like in the past?

Community

12 How do you predict your community will change in the next 10 years?

Community
Question Cards

13 Does your community hold any sort of special events? What type of special events would you like?

14 What services and resources are available to you in your community?

15 If you were designing a newspaper ad to sell houses in your community, what would the ad look like? What would it say?

16 How is a community like a family? How is it different?

Higher-Level Thinking Questions for Social Studies
Kagan Publishing • 1 (800) 933-2667 • www.KaganOnline.com

Community

Journal Writing Question

Write your response to the question below.
Be ready to share your response.

You are nominated as the new chairperson for your community's Improvement Committee. What one thing would you change about your community? Why?

_____
_____
_____
_____
_____
_____
_____
_____
_____
_____
_____
_____
_____
_____
_____
_____
_____
_____
_____

Community

Question Starters

Use the question starters below to create complete questions.
Send your questions to a partner or to another team to answer.

1. How is your community

_____

_____

2. What similarities

_____

_____

3. Who in your community

_____

_____

4. If you lived somewhere else

_____

_____

5. What special features

_____

_____

6. Does your community

_____

_____

7. Are the people in your community

_____

_____

8. How could you improve

_____

_____

Higher-Level Thinking Questions for Social Studies
Kagan Publishing • 1 (800) 933-2667 • www.KaganOnline.com

Cultural
Geography

higher-level thinking questions

"They know enough who know how to learn.

— Henry Adams

Higher-Level Thinking Questions for Social Studies
Kagan Publishing • 1 (800) 933-2667 • www.KaganOnline.com

Cultural Geography
Question Cards

Cultural Geography

1 Both topography and climate have an effect on the activities of a culture. Considering both, what recreational activities might this culture enjoy?

Cultural Geography

2 What might the artwork of this culture look like?

Cultural Geography

3 What does your culture have in common with this culture?

Cultural Geography

4 Why might cultural prejudice be a problem in this area?

Cultural Geography
Question Cards

5 Why might this area be a good place to visit?

6 What values might be important to this culture?

7 Language is constantly changing. Why might the language of this culture have changed over the centuries?

8 Why might someone choose to live in this area?

Higher-Level Thinking Questions for Social Studies
Kagan Publishing • 1 (800) 933-2667 • www.KaganOnline.com

Cultural Geography
Question Cards

Cultural Geography

9 Why might a historian be interested in this culture?

Cultural Geography

10 What type of shelter is suitable for this area? How have homes in this area changed over the centuries?

Cultural Geography

11 Could this area be considered a cultural melting pot? Why or why not?

Cultural Geography

12 How might this culture be different if the area did not have borders?

Cultural Geography
Question Cards

Cultural Geography

13 Imagine yourself on an archaeological dig in the area. What might you find? What would that tell you about the culture?

Cultural Geography

14 What could we learn about the ancient culture of the area from its childrens' toys?

Cultural Geography

15 How does being near or not near a river affect the culture in the area?

Cultural Geography

16 What problems may this culture face 100 years from now?

Higher-Level Thinking Questions for Social Studies
Kagan Publishing • 1 (800) 933-2667 • www.KaganOnline.com

Cultural Geography

Journal Writing Question

Write your response to the question below.
Be ready to share your response.

What does your culture have in common with this culture?

_____
_____
_____
_____
_____
_____
_____
_____
_____
_____
_____
_____
_____
_____
_____
_____
_____
_____
_____
_____

Cultural Geography
Question Starters

Use the question starters below to create complete questions.
Send your questions to a partner or to another team to answer.

1. What impact does

2. If you grew up in this culture

3. What is the relationship

4. What traditions

5. How are the people

6. How might a day

7. What similarities

8. Would you like

Higher-Level Thinking Questions for Social Studies
Kagan Publishing • 1 (800) 933-2667 • www.KaganOnline.com

Culture

higher-level thinking questions

"

All human interactions are opportunities to learn or to teach.

— M. Scott Peck,

The Road Less Traveled

"

Culture
Question Cards

Culture

1 Do you believe one culture is better than another? Or is each culture equally valid in it's own way? Explain.

Culture

2 How would you describe culture to someone who has never heard of it?

Culture

3 Are cultures becoming more similar or different? Explain.

Culture

4 Have you ever had the opportunity to participate in a cultural celebration outside your own culture? If so, describe it. If not, what is one you would enjoy?

Culture

5 Are there some common things that tie all humans together, or is everyone's life completely different depending on their culture? Explain.

Culture

6 If you could introduce or adopt one custom from another culture into your culture, what would it be? Why?

Culture

7 Why do you think people have different customs in their cultures?

Culture

8 Would the world be better or worse if there was just one world culture? Why?

Higher-Level Thinking Questions for Social Studies
Kagan Publishing • 1 (800) 933-2667 • www.KaganOnline.com

Culture
Question Cards

Culture

9 How was culture started? How is it passed on?

Culture

10 What impact does the geography or natural environment have on culture?

Culture

11 How are culture and religion different? How are they similar?

Culture

12 If variety is the spice of life, what is culture? Complete the following sentence: "Culture is..."

Culture
Question Cards

Culture

13 Prejudices and racism stem from ignorance and lack of appreciation of other cultures. What are two things we could do to help people understand and appreciate other cultures?

14 Name three ways your culture differs from other cultures.

15 If you had to eat the food of another culture for the rest of your life, which culture would you choose? Why?

16 What impact does culture have on music and art? Describe one culture and the art and music of the culture.

Higher-Level Thinking Questions for Social Studies
Kagan Publishing • 1 (800) 933-2667 • www.KaganOnline.com

Culture

Journal Writing Question

Write your response to the question below.
Be ready to share your response.

Prejudices and racism stem from ignorance and lack of appreciation of other cultures. What are two things we could do to help people understand and appreciate other cultures?

_____

_____

_____

_____

_____

_____

_____

_____

_____

_____

_____

_____

_____

_____

_____

_____

_____

Culture

Question Starters

Use the question starters below to create complete questions.
Send your questions to a partner or to another team to answer.

1. What role does culture

2. How would you feel if

3. Why are different cultures

4. How could you improve

5. How could you represent

6. What would be different if

7. What is more important

8. Why do people

Higher-Level Thinking Questions for Social Studies
Kagan Publishing • 1 (800) 933-2667 • www.KaganOnline.com

Current Events

higher-level thinking questions

"It is error only, and not truth, that shrinks from inquiry.

— Thomas Paine

Higher-Level Thinking Questions for Social Studies
Kagan Publishing • 1 (800) 933-2667 • www.KaganOnline.com

Current Events
Question Cards

Current Events

1 You are writing a letter to the editor about this topic. What might you say and why?

Current Events

2 Most actions are part of a cause and effect relationship. Do you consider this event or issue to be the "cause" or the "effect"? Explain your opinion.

Current Events

3 What part did modern technology play in this event or issue? How might it change with or without technology?

Current Events

4 Name the most important people involved in this event or issue. How might it be different without them?

Current Events

5 How might this event/issue have been different if it had occurred 100 years ago?

Current Events

6 How are today's morals and values exhibited in this event or issue.

Current Events

7 What might a follow-up story be about?

Current Events

8 History is known to repeat itself. What historical event or issue is similar to this?

Current Events
Question Cards

Current Events

9 Who is most affected by this event or issue? Individual citizens, a particular state, a country or the world? Explain your answer.

Current Events

10 Would you have liked to be a part of this event or issue? Why or why not?

Current Events

11 What other current events or issues are related to this? Explain the relationship.

Current Events

12 What parts of this event or issue are within human control? What parts are controlled by "Mother Nature"?

Current Events
Question Cards

Current Events

13 You have the chance to interview the person(s) involved. What will you ask them?

Current Events

14 How best might this event or issue be dramatized on TV; as a movie, a series, a commercial or a talk show topic?

Current Events

15 Complete the following analogy: This event or issue is like a

_____

because_____.

Current Events

16 Could this event or issue occur in another country with a different government? Why or why not?

Higher-Level Thinking Questions for Social Studies
Kagan Publishing • 1 (800) 933-2667 • www.KaganOnline.com

Current Events

Journal Writing Question

Write your response to the question below.
Be ready to share your response.

How best might this event or issue be dramatized on TV; as a movie, a series, a commercial or a talk show topic?

Current Events

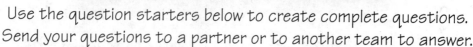
Question Starters

Use the question starters below to create complete questions.
Send your questions to a partner or to another team to answer.

1. What is the importance of

_____

_____

2. Who is

_____

_____

3. How might

_____

_____

4. When would

_____

_____

5. What can

_____

_____

6. What would

_____

_____

7. How do you feel

_____

8. Does this event

_____

Higher-Level Thinking Questions for Social Studies
Kagan Publishing • 1 (800) 933-2667 • www.KaganOnline.com

Economic Geography

higher-level thinking questions

I thought so hard
I got a headache.

— J. D. Cobb

Higher-Level Thinking Questions for Social Studies
Kagan Publishing • 1 (800) 933-2667 • www.KaganOnline.com

Economic Geography
Question Cards

Economic Geography

1 How else might the natural resources of the area be used?

Economic Geography

2 How might the economy of the area change in the next 100 years?

Economic Geography

3 What can you tell about the soil in the area?

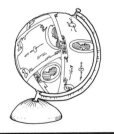

Economic Geography

4 How does the location of the area allow for barter and trade?

Economic Geography
Question Cards

Economic Geography

5 What might the people of the area need to import?

Economic Geography

6 Explain how the location of the area may have affected its economic growth.

Economic Geography

7 What tools might the area's ancient culture have used?

Economic Geography

8 How would the economy be affected if the area's natural resources were used up?

Higher-Level Thinking Questions for Social Studies
Kagan Publishing • 1 (800) 933-2667 • www.KaganOnline.com

Economic Geography
Question Cards

Economic Geography

9 Could the climate of the area be considered a natural resource? Why or why not?

Economic Geography

10 Is this area an important center for trade? Explain why or why not.

Economic Geography

11 How does being near or not near a water source affect the economy of the area?

Economic Geography

12 How has communication with other areas affected the economic growth of the area?

Economic Geography
Question Cards

13 What events might threaten the economy of the area?

14 What might an economist say about the area?

15 What types of technology may improve the economy of the area?

16 What skills might a person need to work in the area?

Higher-Level Thinking Questions for Social Studies
Kagan Publishing • 1 (800) 933-2667 • www.KaganOnline.com

Economic Geography

Journal Writing Question

Write your response to the question below.
Be ready to share your response.

Explain how the location of the area may have affected its economic growth.

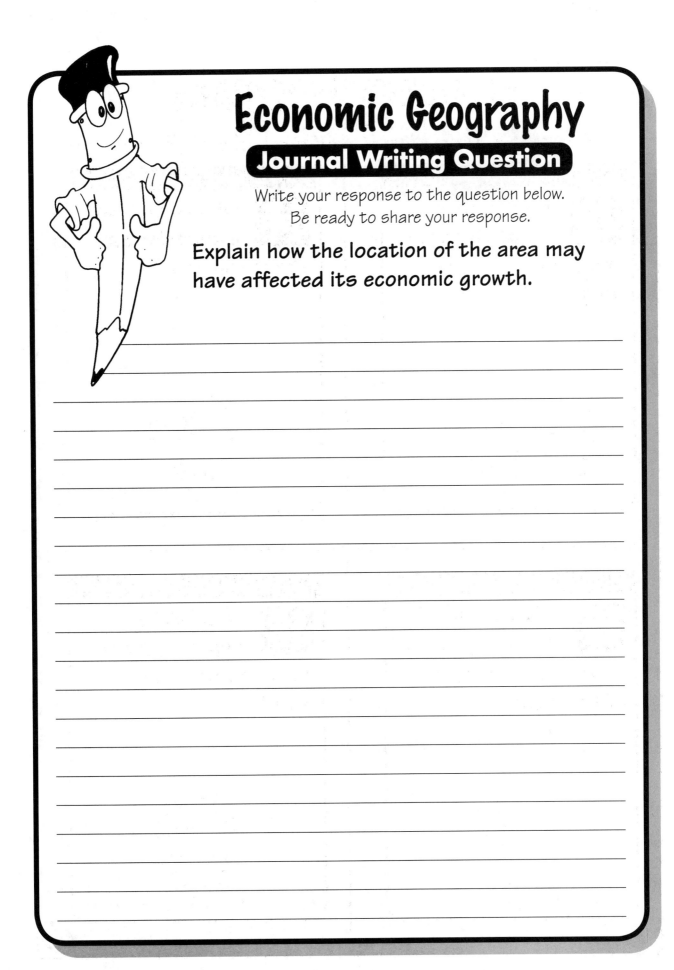

_____
_____
_____
_____
_____
_____
_____
_____
_____
_____
_____
_____
_____
_____
_____
_____
_____
_____
_____
_____
_____

Economic Geography
Question Starters

Use the question starters below to create complete questions.
Send your questions to a partner or to another team to answer.

1. How would you describe

2. If you had to choose

3. How could you improve

4. What do you predict

5. Why is the economy

6. What factors influence

7. If you lived in this region

8. What problems

Higher-Level Thinking Questions for Social Studies
Kagan Publishing • 1 (800) 933-2667 • www.KaganOnline.com

Explorers

higher-level thinking questions

"One doesn't discover new lands without consenting to lose sight of the shore for a very long time.

— André Gide

Higher-Level Thinking Questions for Social Studies
Kagan Publishing • 1 (800) 933-2667 • www.KaganOnline.com

Explorers
Question Cards

Explorers

1 How is exploration by ship in the past like space exploration today? How is it different?

Explorers

2 Have you ever done any exploration? If so, describe where and what it was like. Where else would you like to explore?

Explorers

3 What are three qualities a good explorer should have? Why?

Explorers

4 When Hernando Cortés came to Mexico in 1519 he took Aztecs prisoners, killed many in battles and stole their gold. Why did some explorers conquer the natives and destroy their cultures while others were more peaceful?

Explorers
Question Cards

5 If you were an explorer of the past, what would you say to convince the king or queen to finance your expedition?

6 If you were an explorer who found a culture with many riches, and you knew you could defeat the people and get their treasures, would you? Why or why not?

7 How would you feel if someone invaded your land, killed your family and friends, and made you a slave in your own land?

8 Many explorers became famous for their explorations. What would you like to be known for?

Higher-Level Thinking Questions for Social Studies
Kagan Publishing • 1 (800) 933-2667 • www.KaganOnline.com

Explorers
Question Cards

Explorers

9 It is a myth that Columbus set off to prove the world was round. Educated people in his time already knew it was round. Why do you think so many myths exist about history?

Explorers

10 You want to explore a new land, but it will be very risky and you will need a large crew. What can you say to bring others on board?

Explorers

11 If you were the head of an exploration and your food was running out, people on your crew were dying of illnesses, and you ran into bad weather, would you turn back knowing you may never have the opportunity again?

Explorers

12 Would you rather explore by land, air or sea? Explain why.

Explorers
Question Cards

Explorers

13 How would you feel seeing land after a long and hard journey by sea? What would be some of the first things you would do?

Explorers

14 What would motivate an explorer to take the risk of a dangerous journey?

Explorers

15 If you could be any explorer, which would you be? Why?

Explorers

16 What explorer had the biggest impact on us today? Why?

Higher-Level Thinking Questions for Social Studies
Kagan Publishing • 1 (800) 933-2667 • www.KaganOnline.com

Explorers

Write your response to the question below.
Be ready to share your response.

Have you ever done any exploration? If so, describe where and what it was like. Where else would you like to explore?

_____

_____

_____

_____

_____

_____

_____

_____

_____

_____

_____

_____

_____

_____

_____

_____

_____

_____

_____

_____

_____

Explorers

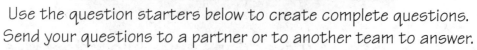
Question Starters

Use the question starters below to create complete questions.
Send your questions to a partner or to another team to answer.

1. What would be different if _____

_____

2. What caused _____

_____

3. Which explorer _____

_____

4. If you were an explorer _____

_____

5. Would you rather _____

_____

6. Where _____

_____

7. How could you describe _____

_____

8. How could you categorize _____

_____

Higher-Level Thinking Questions for Social Studies
Kagan Publishing • 1 (800) 933-2667 • www.KaganOnline.com

Family

higher-level thinking questions

"Education is what survives when what has been learnt has been forgotten.

— B. F. Skinner

Higher-Level Thinking Questions for Social Studies
Kagan Publishing • 1 (800) 933-2667 • www.KaganOnline.com

Family
Question Cards

Family
1 How would your life be different if you didn't have a family?

Family
2 Does your family have any special traditions? If so, describe them. If not, what would you like to do as a family tradition?

Family
3 How is your family like other families? How is your family unique?

Family
4 What is your favorite thing you do with your family? When did you do it last and what was it like?

Family
Question Cards

5 Do you consider yourself close to your grandparents? Why or why not?

6 In the past and in other cultures children, parents, grandparents, great grandparents, aunts, uncles, and cousins lived under the same roof. Describe three advantages and three disadvantages of living with your extended family.

7 Do people have to be connected by blood to be family? Why or why not?

8 Why do you think more married couples get divorced now than in the past? How does a divorce affect the family?

Higher-Level Thinking Questions for Social Studies
Kagan Publishing • 1 (800) 933-2667 • www.KaganOnline.com

Family
Question Cards

Family

9 What responsibilities do you have in your family? Would you like to have more or fewer responsibilities?

Family

10 If you could change one thing about your family, what would it be? Why?

Family

11 Are you more like your mother or more like your father? Why do you say so?

Family

12 Do you plan on getting married and having children? If so, when and how many children? If not, why not?

Family
Question Cards

Family

13 In what ways are members of your family similar? In what ways is each person unique? Explain.

Family

14 Do you think people are the way they are because of their genes or because of the way they were brought up?

Family

15 What is the history and or the meaning of your last name (also called your family name)? If you don't know, how could you find out?

Family

16 Do you ever fight with anyone in your family? If so, who do you fight with and why? If not, how do you keep the peace?

Higher-Level Thinking Questions for Social Studies
Kagan Publishing • 1 (800) 933-2667 • www.KaganOnline.com

Family

Journal Writing Question

Write your response to the question below.
Be ready to share your response.

Are you more like your mother or more like your father? Why do you say so?

_____

_____

_____

_____

_____

_____

_____

_____

_____

_____

_____

_____

_____

_____

_____

_____

_____

_____

_____

Family

Question Starters

Use the question starters below to create complete questions.
Send your questions to a partner or to another team to answer.

1. If your family _____
_____

2. What would it be like _____
_____

3. What customs _____
_____

4. What is the most memorable _____
_____

5. How could you describe _____
_____

6. Who in your family _____
_____

7. If you had to choose _____
_____

8. Why is it important _____
_____

Higher-Level Thinking Questions for Social Studies
Kagan Publishing • 1 (800) 933-2667 • www.KaganOnline.com

Government
Issues

higher-level thinking questions

"

We the people of the United States, in order to form a more perfect Union, establish justice, ensure domestic tranquility, provide for the common defense, promote the general welfare, and secure the blessings of liberty to ourselves and our posterity, do ordain and establish this Constitution for the United States of America.

— Preamble,

The Constitution of the United States

"

Higher-Level Thinking Questions for Social Studies
Kagan Publishing • 1 (800) 933-2667 • www.KaganOnline.com

Government Issues
Question Cards

1 If the president commits perjury (lies under oath), should he or she be removed from office? Why or why not?

2 Do you think the rich should pay more taxes than the poor? Describe your position.

3 If a terrorist commits a crime against our country and we know who it is, what should we do?

4 Do you think war is ever warranted? If so, when? If not, why not?

Government Issues
Question Cards

Government Issues

5 Some people running for a government office have a lot of money to spend on their campaign, while others have much less. Do you think this is fair? What could we do to make running for office more fair?

Government Issues

6 Should the government ever have the right to spy on people? If so, when? If not, why not?

Government Issues

7 The Constitution grants citizens the right to bear arms. Do you think people should be allowed to own and carry guns today? Why or why not?

Government Issues

8 Democrats and Republicans are the two major political parties in our country. What are the differences in their beliefs?

Higher-Level Thinking Questions for Social Studies
Kagan Publishing • 1 (800) 933-2667 • www.KaganOnline.com

Government Issues
Question Cards

Government Issues

9 In the time of the Prohibition, alcohol was illegal. Crime and violence followed. Today there is crime and violence related to illegal drugs. Do you think drugs should be legalized? Describe your position.

Government Issues

10 Should our borders be open to anyone who wants to come to our country, or should there be restrictions? Explain.

Government Issues

11 Do you think that we should have a death penalty? If so, when should a person be sentenced to death?

Government Issues

12 What would happen if there was no organized government?

Government Issues
Question Cards

Government Issues

13 If another country invades a smaller, weaker country, do you think the United States should get involved?

Government Issues

14 In our country there is a separation between church and state. That means religion and government are separate. Is this good or bad? Explain.

Government Issues

15 Complete the following sentence. "Democracy is..."

Government Issues

16 Do you think people should be allowed to say and publish anything they want or should the government set restrictions on people's freedom of speech?

Higher-Level Thinking Questions for Social Studies
Kagan Publishing • 1 (800) 933-2667 • www.KaganOnline.com

Government Issues

Journal Writing Question

Write your response to the question below.
Be ready to share your response.

The Constitution grants citizens the right to bear arms. Do you think people should be allowed to own and carry guns today? Why or why not?

_____

_____

_____

_____

_____

_____

_____

_____

_____

_____

_____

_____

_____

_____

_____

_____

_____

_____

_____

Government Issues
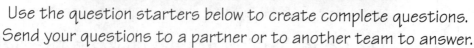
Question Starters

Use the question starters below to create complete questions.
Send your questions to a partner or to another team to answer.

1. What are some solutions

_____

_____

2. Which issue

_____

_____

3. How does our government compare

_____

_____

4. If you were the president

_____

_____

5. Is democracy

_____

_____

6. In the future, do you think

_____

_____

 7. How could you improve

_____

_____

8. If you could vote

_____

_____

Higher-Level Thinking Questions for Social Studies
Kagan Publishing • 1 (800) 933-2667 • www.KaganOnline.com

Historical Characters

higher-level thinking questions

One man that has a mind and knows it can always beat ten men who haven't and don't.

— George Bernard Shaw

Higher-Level Thinking Questions for Social Studies
Kagan Publishing • 1 (800) 933-2667 • www.KaganOnline.com

Historical Character
Question Cards

Historical Character

1 If the character were alive now, what might he or she accomplish today?

Historical Character

2 How is this character like or unlike you?

Historical Character

3 This character has come back to visit the president of the United States. What advice might the character give him or her?

Historical Character

4 How might the world be different today if this character never lived?

Historical Character
Question Cards

Historical Character

5 One's values are revealed by one's actions. What is the most important value reflected by the actions of this person?

Historical Character

6 Consider the accomplishments of this character. If you were this character, of what accomplishment would you be most proud? Why?

Historical Character

7 If you could ask this person two questions, what would they be?

Historical Character

8 This person has been granted three wishes to change today's world. What might they be?

Higher-Level Thinking Questions for Social Studies
Kagan Publishing • 1 (800) 933-2667 • www.KaganOnline.com

Historical Character
Question Cards

Historical Character

9 If there were one action of this person you could change, which would it be? Why?

Historical Character

10 Describe the physical characteristics of this person. If you could change one, which one would you change? Why?

Historical Character

11 If the character took a two week vacation today, where might he or she choose to go and why?

Historical Character

12 You have been granted one day to go back in history to become this person. What would you do differently?

Historical Character
Question Cards

13 Suppose this person were transported to the middle of World War 2 (WWII). What role might he or she play?

14 This person sits at home alone writing in a diary. He or she starts to write, "The one thing that bothers me most..." Complete the idea and explain why.

15 You have been granted special powers that make you invisible and let you travel through time. What event in the life of the character would you choose to observe?

16 You have opened a letter written to this character's best friend. It says, "My greatest regret is..." Finish this sentence.

112

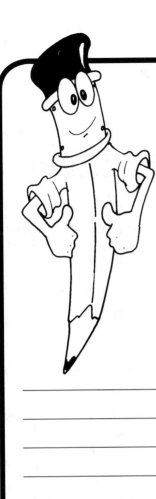

Historical Character

Journal Writing Question

Write your response to the question below.
Be ready to share your response.

Consider the accomplishments of this character. If you were this character, of what accomplishment would you be most proud? Why?

_____

_____

_____

_____

_____

_____

_____

_____

_____

_____

_____

_____

_____

_____

_____

_____

Historical Character
Question Starters

Use the question starters below to create complete questions.
Send your questions to a partner or to another team to answer.

1. At what point

_____

_____

2. What characteristics

_____

_____

3. If you were this character

_____

_____

4. What is another way

_____

_____

5. What social problems

_____

_____

6. What influence

_____

_____

7. Do you admire

_____

_____

8. How could you summarize

_____

_____

Higher-Level Thinking Questions for Social Studies
Kagan Publishing • 1 (800) 933-2667 • www.KaganOnline.com

Historical Event

higher-level thinking questions

"The most important thing in raising a child is not to try to put the stamp of the past on that child, but to give that child the freedom to grow and explore...

— Catherine Bateson

Historical Event
Question Cards

Historical Event	**Historical Event**
1 Explain what the situation was immediately before the event took place. 	**2** Would you like to have been a part of this event? Why or why not? 
Historical Event	**Historical Event**
3 Who were the most important people involved in the event? 	**4** Imagine yourself involved in this event. What information would you include in a letter home? 

Historical Event

5 Explain what the situation was immediately following the event.

Historical Event

6 Imagine you were a reporter assigned to cover this event. Describe what you saw and heard.

Historical Event

7 If an artist were hired to paint a scene of the event, what single scene best representing the event do you think the artist should depict?

Historical Event

8 Suppose this event were being made into a movie. Would it be a comedy, drama, action/adventure or a horror movie? Explain.

Higher-Level Thinking Questions for Social Studies
Kagan Publishing • 1 (800) 933-2667 • www.KaganOnline.com

Historical Event
Question Cards

Historical Event

9 What affect did this event have on the history of the world?

Historical Event

10 Suppose a picture of the event were in the newspaper. What might the caption under the picture say?

Historical Event

11 If you could change part or all of this event, what would you change and why?

Historical Event

12 How have the results of this event ultimately affected your life and/ or family?

Historical Event
Question Cards

Historical Event

13 How might this event have been different if it occurred today?

Historical Event

14 Pretend a memorial were going to be built in honor of this historical event. What might it look like and why?

Historical Event

15 What could have happened to change the outcome of the event?

Historical Event

16 How might a change in the weather have affected the event?

Higher-Level Thinking Questions for Social Studies
Kagan Publishing • 1 (800) 933-2667 • www.KaganOnline.com

Historical Event

Journal Writing Question

Write your response to the question below.
Be ready to share your response.

Imagine you were a reporter assigned to cover this event. Describe what you saw and heard.

Historical Event

Question Starters

Use the question starters below to create complete questions.
Send your questions to a partner or to another team to answer.

1. How has this event
_____
_____

2. What would be different if
_____
_____

3. If you were alive
_____
_____

4. How could you represent
_____
_____

5. What is the moral
_____
_____

6. How would you feel if
_____
_____

7. Could this event
_____
_____

8. Why is it important
_____
_____

Higher-Level Thinking Questions for Social Studies
Kagan Publishing • 1 (800) 933-2667 • www.KaganOnline.com

Holidays

higher-level thinking questions

Each thought that is welcomed and recorded is a nest egg by the side of which more will be laid.

— Henry David Thoreau

Higher-Level Thinking Questions for Social Studies
Kagan Publishing • 1 (800) 933-2667 • www.KaganOnline.com

Holidays
Question Cards

Holidays

1 What is your favorite holiday? Why is it your favorite?

Holidays

2 How are Halloween and Easter similar? How are they different?

Holidays

3 Make up a new holiday you think everyone should celebrate. What is it called? When is it celebrated? What do people do to celebrate it?

Holidays

4 Why do different cultures have different holidays with different types of ceremonies?

Holidays
Question Cards

5 When you think of Christmas, what comes to mind?

6 Can you think of another cultures' holiday that we celebrate? Why do you think we celebrate it here?

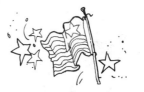

7 Why do we celebrate St. Valentine's Day? What does February 14th mean to you?

8 Why do we celebrate George Washington's and Abe Lincoln's birthdays, but not the birthdays of any other presidents?

Higher-Level Thinking Questions for Social Studies
Kagan Publishing • 1 (800) 933-2667 • www.KaganOnline.com

Holidays
Question Cards

Holidays

9 What is your favorite part about Thanksgiving? What special things does your family do to celebrate?

Holidays

10 The fourth of July is Independence Day. What does freedom mean to you?

Holidays

11 If we have a Mother's Day and a Father's day, should we also have a Son's Day and Daughter's Day? Why or why not?

Holidays

12 Out of all the famous people in our history, why do you think we chose to celebrate Martin Luther King, Jr.?

Holidays
Question Cards

Holidays

13 Do you prefer Easter or Thanksgiving? Why?

Holidays

14 The word "Holiday" is made up of two shorter words put together. Why do you think those two words are put together?

Holidays

15 If you had to do without one holiday, which would it be? Why?

Holidays

16 What would the year be like without any holidays?

Higher-Level Thinking Questions for Social Studies
Kagan Publishing • 1 (800) 933-2667 • www.KaganOnline.com

Holidays

Journal Writing Question

Write your response to the question below.
Be ready to share your response.

Make up a new holiday you think everyone should celebrate. What is it called? When is it celebrated? What do people do to celebrate it?

_____

_____

_____

_____

_____

_____

_____

_____

_____

_____

_____

_____

_____

_____

_____

_____

Holidays
Question Starters

Use the question starters below to create complete questions.
Send your questions to a partner or to another team to answer.

1. How are holidays

2. Is Christmas

3. Why have we chosen

4. What is the importance of

5. Which holiday is most like

6. Would you rather

7. What common characteristics

8. Should we celebrate

Higher-Level Thinking Questions for Social Studies
Kagan Publishing • 1 (800) 933-2667 • www.KaganOnline.com

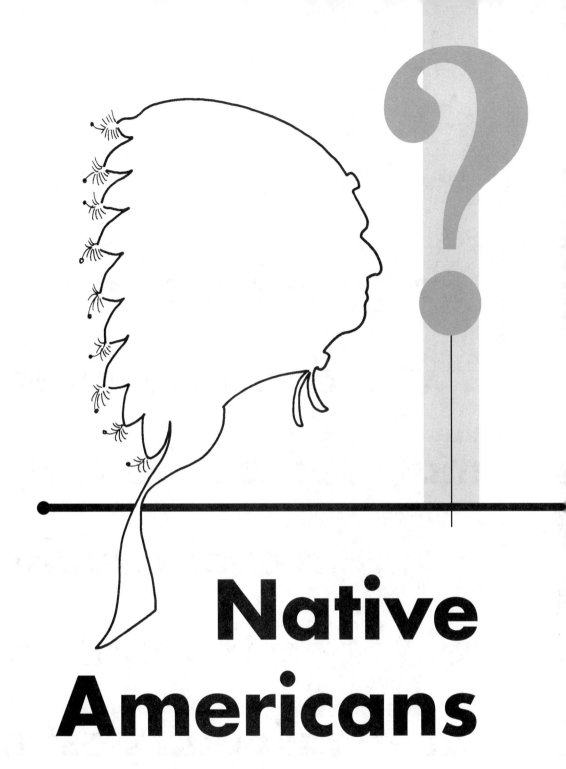

Native Americans

higher-level thinking questions

"Every event that a man would master must be mounted on the run, and no man ever caught the reins of a thought except as it galloped past him.

— Oliver Wendell Holmes

Higher-Level Thinking Questions for Social Studies
Kagan Publishing • 1 (800) 933-2667 • www.KaganOnline.com

Native Americans
Question Cards

Native Americans

1 Do you think it is fair that Native Americans can make their own laws on reservations such as having casinos in states where gambling is illegal? Why or why not?

Native Americans

2 When Christopher Columbus sailed to the New World he thought he reached the Indies and called the people there Indians. Why do you think the term "Native Americans" is preferred today?

Native Americans

3 If Native Americans lived in the United States and Canada long before Christopher Columbus, why do you think we often say he "discovered" America in 1492?

Native Americans

4 What do you think the landscape looked like 400 years ago, in the time Native Americans prevailed? Describe it in as much detail as possible.

Native Americans
Question Cards

Native Americans

5 Native Americans were much happier than we are today because they were so close to nature. Do you agree or disagree?

Native Americans

6 If you were going to be given a Native American name such as Dancing Squirrel, what name would you want? Why?

Native Americans

7 Native Americans often wore face paint for special ceremonies. Do we have any similar practices today? Explain.

Native Americans

8 Native Americans lived in tribes like the Ojibwa, Cree, Powhatan, Iroquois, Sioux, Nootka, Hopi, Cherokee, Navajo. Do we have anything like tribes today? Describe.

Higher-Level Thinking Questions for Social Studies
Kagan Publishing • 1 (800) 933-2667 • www.KaganOnline.com

Native Americans
Question Cards

Native Americans

9 How are Native Americans portrayed on TV and in the movies? Do you think it is an accurate picture?

Native Americans

10 Native Americans used totem poles to tell their clan's history. What would your family's totem pole look like?

Native Americans

11 What impact did geographical location have on Native American customs?

Native Americans

12 How is eating different for us today than it was for Native Americans in the past?

Native Americans
Question Cards

Native Americans

13 America wasn't discovered, it was stolen from the Native Americans. Do you agree or disagree with this statement?

Native Americans

14 When the Pilgrims came to America, half of them died from the harsh first winter. Squanto, a Native American, became friends with the Pilgrims and showed them good places to hunt, fish, and how to plant crops. The Pilgrims had a Thanksgiving feast to show their gratitude to Native Americans. Why do you think relations were not always so positive?

Native Americans

15 Would you rather live in the time of Native Americans or now? Explain your answer.

Native Americans

16 If you could be a member of one Native American tribe, which tribe would you choose? Why?

Higher-Level Thinking Questions for Social Studies
Kagan Publishing • 1 (800) 933-2667 • www.KaganOnline.com

Native Americans

Journal Writing Question

Write your response to the question below.
Be ready to share your response.

America wasn't discovered, it was stolen from the Native Americans. Do you agree or disagree with this statement?

_____

_____

_____

_____

_____

_____

_____

_____

_____

_____

_____

_____

_____

_____

_____

_____

Native Americans
Question Starters

Use the question starters below to create complete questions.
Send your questions to a partner or to another team to answer.

1. How can you explain

2. If you were a Native American

3. What similarities

4. What symbol best represents

5. What was the relationship

6. Why is it important

7. What problems

8. In the future,

Higher-Level Thinking Questions for Social Studies
Kagan Publishing • 1 (800) 933-2667 • www.KaganOnline.com

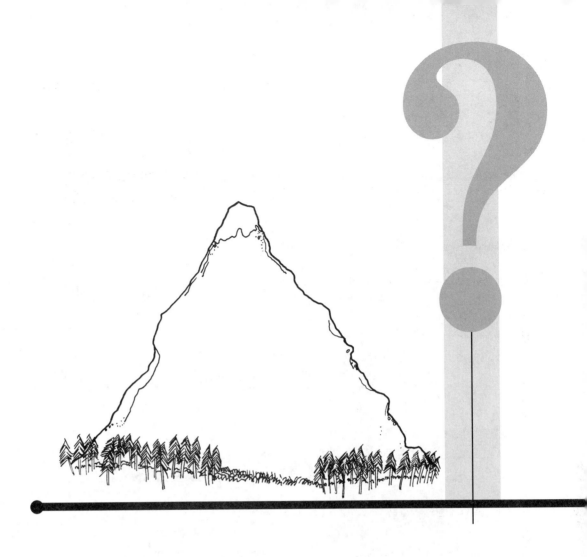

Physical Geography

higher-level thinking questions

"Thought takes man out of servitude, into freedom."

— Henry Wadsworth Longfellow

Physical Geography
Question Cards

Physical Geography

1 Which methods of transportation are best suited for the area?

Physical Geography

2 What information could you give to describe the area's exact location on a map?

Physical Geography

3 Some scientists believe the earth once had one large continent. What present day countries might then have bordered the area?

Physical Geography

4 How might you describe the area to a blind person?

Physical Geography
Question Cards

5 Describe a landscape an artist might paint of the area.

6 How have the people in the area adapted to the physical environment?

7 How has the area been affected by natural disasters?

8 Is the area more horizontal or vertical? Describe.

Higher-Level Thinking Questions for Social Studies
Kagan Publishing • 1 (800) 933-2667 • www.KaganOnline.com

Physical Geography
Question Cards

9 Why might you find sea shells on the area's highest elevation point?

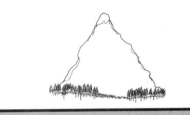

10 Choose one word to describe the climate of the area. Describe your word choice.

11 What type of natural disasters occur in the area? Why?

12 How does the distance from the equator affect the climate of the area?

Physical Geography
Question Cards

13 How would life be different without the animals that live in the area?

14 How are the plants of the area suited to live there?

15 What other area has similar landforms?

16 From the area's highest point, what might you see?

Higher-Level Thinking Questions for Social Studies
Kagan Publishing • 1 (800) 933-2667 • www.KaganOnline.com

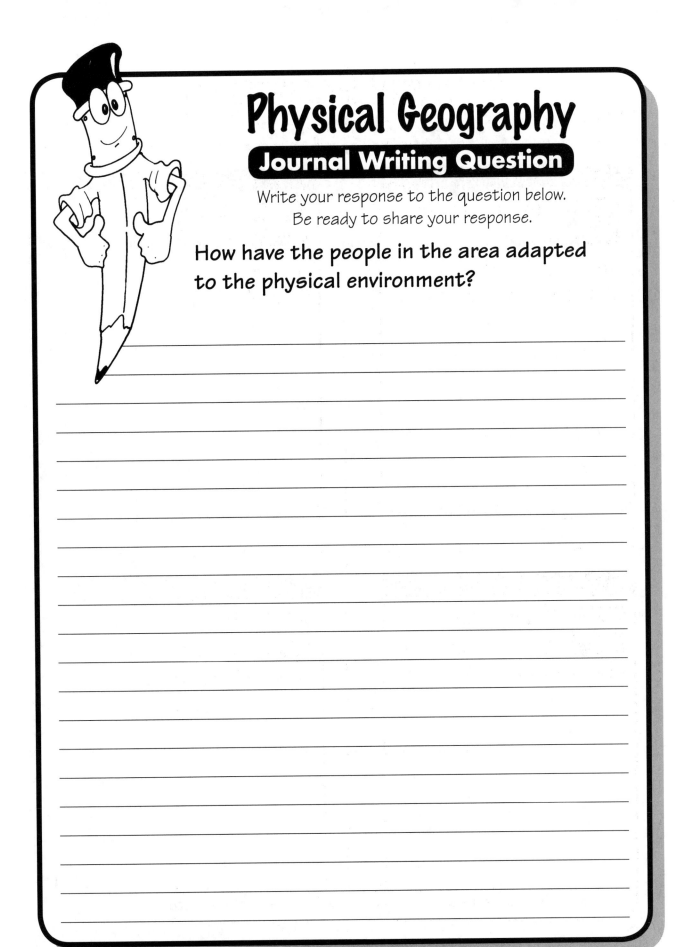

Physical Geography
Journal Writing Question

Write your response to the question below.
Be ready to share your response.

How have the people in the area adapted to the physical environment?

Physical Geography

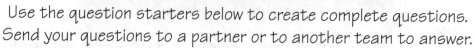

Question Starters

Use the question starters below to create complete questions.
Send your questions to a partner or to another team to answer.

1. What influence

2. If you could visit

3. How could you describe

4. What would be different if

5. What adaptations

6. Why

7. What special features

8. What is the relationship

Higher-Level Thinking Questions for Social Studies
Kagan Publishing • 1 (800) 933-2667 • www.KaganOnline.com

Religion

higher-level thinking questions

Question with boldness even the existence of a God; because, if there be one, he must more approve of the homage of reason, than that of blindfolded fear.

— Thomas Jefferson

Higher-Level Thinking Questions for Social Studies
Kagan Publishing • 1 (800) 933-2667 • www.KaganOnline.com

Religion
Question Cards

Religion

1 Why do you think different people have different religious beliefs?

Religion

2 There are many religions in the world. Do you think there is one right religion?

Religion

3 What are some things all religions have in common? Explain.

Religion

4 Why do you think so many wars have been fought over religion?

Religion
Question Cards

Religion

5 Why is it important that freedom of religion is included in the first amendment of the Constitution? Explain.

Religion

6 Name three holidays we celebrate that are based on religious beliefs. Why do you think our country recognizes the holidays of some religions but not the holidays of other religions?

Religion

7 Do you think religion has more to do with beliefs or with customs? Explain.

Religion

8 Why do you think some people are very religious while others are not religious at all?

Higher-Level Thinking Questions for Social Studies
Kagan Publishing • 1 (800) 933-2667 • www.KaganOnline.com

Religion
Question Cards

Religion

9 Complete the following statement. "Religion is..."

Religion

10 How would the world be different if there were no religions?

Religion

11 How is religion like culture? How is it different?

Religion

12 Do you think prayer should be allowed in public school? Why or why not?

Religion

13 How would you feel if you were persecuted for your religious beliefs? Why do you think people have been persecuted throughout history?

Religion

14 What are some advantages of religion?

Religion

15 Where did you get your religious beliefs?

Religion

16 In the past, people would offer sacrifices, (sometimes even human sacrifices) to the gods. Do people still practice religious sacrifices in some form today?

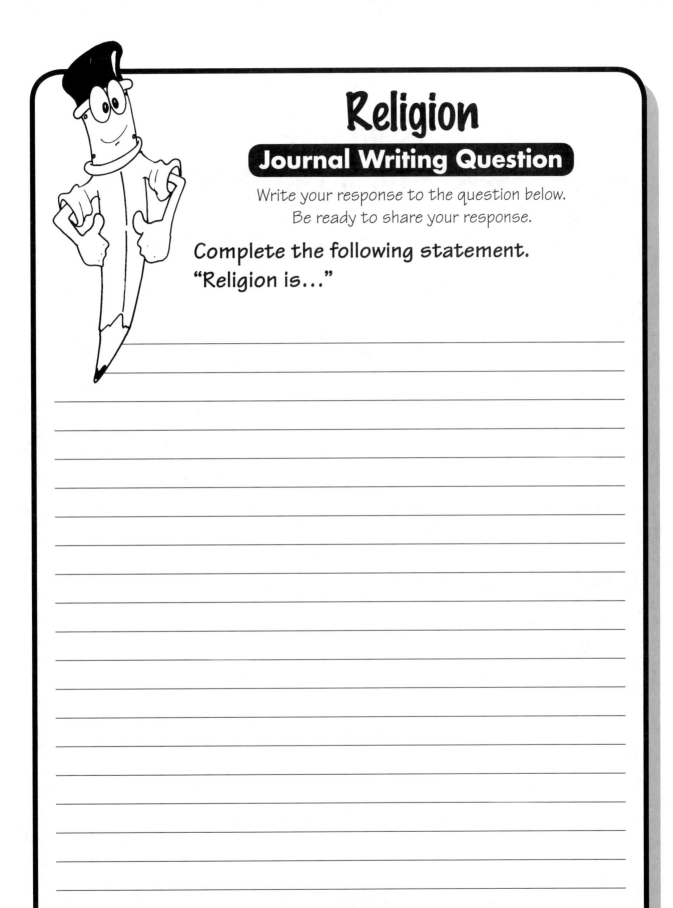

Religion

Journal Writing Question

Write your response to the question below.
Be ready to share your response.

**Complete the following statement.
"Religion is..."**

Religion

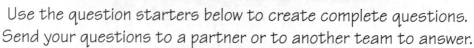
Use the question starters below to create complete questions.
Send your questions to a partner or to another team to answer.

1. Why is religion
_____
_____

2. How could you learn more about
_____
_____

3. What are some different opinions
_____
_____

4. What do you wonder about
_____
_____

5. If you could ask one
_____
_____

6. Should people
_____
_____

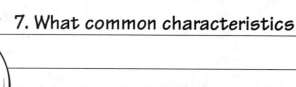
7. What common characteristics
_____

8. What would be different if
_____
_____

Higher-Level Thinking Questions for Social Studies
Kagan Publishing • 1 (800) 933-2667 • www.KaganOnline.com